A Guide to

A Guide to

Zen

Lessons from a Modern Master

Katsuki Sekida

Edited by Marc Allen

NEW WORLD LIBRARY
NOVATO, CALIFORNIA

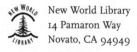

New World Library
14 Pamaron Way
Novato, CA 94949

This condensed edition © 2003 Marc Allen. Condensed from *Zen Training* by Katsuki Sekida © 1975 Katsuki Sekida and A. V. Grimstone. Published by Weatherhill, Inc., 568 Broadway, Suite 705, New York, NY 10012

Text design: Tona Pearce Myers

Library of Congress Cataloging-in-Publication Data
Sekida, Katsuki, 1903–1987.
  A guide to Zen : lessons from a modern master / Katsuki Sekida ; edited by Marc Allen.
      p.   cm.
Includes bibliographical references and index.
ISBN 978-1-57731-249-9 (hardcover : alk. paper)
1. Zen meditations. I. Allen, Mark, 1946– II. Title.
BQ9289.5.S45 2003
294.3'4435—dc21   2003009158

First printing of paperback edition, February 2013
ISBN 978-1-60868-171-6
Printed in Canada on 100% postconsumer-waste recycled paper

New World Library is proud to be a Gold Certified Environmentally Responsible Publisher. Publisher certification awarded by Green Press Initiative. www.greenpressinitiative.org

10   9   8   7   6   5   4   3   2

CONTENTS

I HAVE MET TWO MASTERS of Zen meditation in my life. If you have met only one, you have been fortunate, for one who understands Zen is able to show us, easily and effortlessly, the power and beauty of Zen.

The first was Suzuki Roshi, the founder of the San Francisco Zen Center. The second was Katsuki

Sekida, when he taught in the early 1970s at the Maui Zendo in Hawaii. There were many similarities between them: Both were older men with great physical energy and a passion for Zen, and both had an extraordinary ocean of calmness about them as well — an unchanging serenity that had no bounds.

Both were undoubtedly masters, though Katsuki Sekida would probably smile and deny it if he were called that. He used to deny that he was even a teacher of Zen. He was just a layman, he said modestly. But it was undeniable, with every word and every action, that he was a great teacher. He spoke and wrote from the experience of many, many years of deep *samadhi,* beginning when he was quite young.

The work of both men — the talks of Suzuki Roshi and the writings of Katsuki Sekida — resulted in a few powerful books. Suzuki Roshi's *Zen Mind, Beginner's Mind* is excellent; so is his relatively recent book *Not Always So: Practicing the True Spirit of Zen.*

Katsuki Sekida's *Zen Training,* first published in 1975, remains a classic, one of the most comprehensive guides to Zen ever written, and his other great

work, *Two Zen Classics*, consists of Sekida's transla-
tion and commentary on the koans — the enigmatic
puzzles, the brief stories studied by the Rinzai school
of Zen, one of the main schools of Zen Buddhism.
Both books are endless sources of insight and wisdom. I will continue to study both for the rest of
my life.

I stayed at the Maui Zendo for nearly six
months, and came to know and love Katsuki
Sekida. He meditated with us morning, noon, and
night, and while the rest of us worked in the late
morning and afternoon in the garden or kitchen or
in construction of a new building, he first did a vigorous series of physical exercises, then took a
vigorous walk, swinging his arms wildly and
widely, and then he sat perfectly straight on a stool
and wrote for hours at a stretch, longhand, on big
sheets of unlined paper set on an artist's easel.

For several months, it was my job to type up his
words. His writing was small and clear, in perfectly
straight lines across the page. His English was
lucid and impeccable. Though he had been born
and spent almost all his life in Japan, he wrote bet-
ter English than most native-born Americans. He
was seventy-seven years old when I knew him, and

he had more energy than most of us there — and the majority of us were in our early twenties. His light was always on late into the night — often until 2:30 A.M. or so — and he was usually sitting on his stool, back perfectly straight, writing. Then he would get up and meditate with the rest of us at 5:30 A.M.

The articles he wrote at the time were eventually incorporated into his great work, *Zen Training*. The book is over 100,000 words long, and can be daunting at first to many readers. I've often thought a smaller, condensed version of the book would be welcome to many readers and students of Zen, including myself, and when I approached the good people at Weatherhill, the publishers of both of Katsuki Sekida's books, they enthusiastically gave their permission and support for the project.

And so once again, after more than thirty years, I find myself typing up Katsuki Sekida's writing. It's a great honor. I'm delighted to be able to spend so much time with his words, and offer you the gems that seem particularly shining. He attained deep *samadhi* in his meditation, and he carried it through every moment of his life. His words are written from the very depths of meditation, and can lead us to those depths.

I have lightly edited his words at times, usually condensing longer sentences into shorter ones, occasionally selecting simpler or clearer words or phrases. I have edited slowly and carefully — the only possible way to edit words of such depth and power — and hope that I have conveyed the spirit of the original in every sentence. Please forgive any errors or omissions I have made; if things aren't absolutely clear to you in these pages, or if you want to explore more deeply the great original work these words are taken from, please pick up and study *Zen Training*. It is a masterpiece.

I pray that this book helps you in your understanding of Zen. I pray that it touches you and affects the quality of your life in countless miraculous ways.

Marc Allen
Spring 2003

CHAPTER ONE

A Summary at the

$\mathcal{B}$eginning

Zen is not, in my view, philosophy or mysticism.
It is simply a practice of readjustment of
nervous activity. That is, it restores the distorted
nervous system to its normal functioning.

IN STUDYING ZEN, WE START WITH PRACTICE

Now, it is true that Zen is concerned with the problem of the nature of mind, so it necessarily includes an element of philosophical speculation. However, while most philosophy relies mainly on speculation and reason, in Zen we are never separated from our personal practice, which we carry out with our body and mind.

The basic kind of Zen practice is called *zazen* (sitting Zen), and in zazen we attain *samadhi*. In this state the activity of consciousness is stopped and we cease to be aware of time, space, and causation. It may at first sight seem to be nothing more than mere being, or existence, but if you really attain this state you will find it to be a remarkable thing.

We reach a state in which absolute silence and stillness reign, bathed in a pure, serene light. But it is not a vacuum or mere nothingness. There is a definite wakefulness in it. It recalls the impressive silence and stillness that we experience in the heart of the mountains.

IN ORDINARY DAILY LIFE our consciousness works ceaselessly to protect and maintain our interests. It has acquired the habit of "utilitarian thinking" — looking upon the things in the world as so many tools, looking at objects in the light of how they can be made use of. We call this attitude the habitual way of consciousness. This way of looking at things is the origin of our distorted view of the world.

We come to see ourselves, too, as objects to be made use of, and we fail to see into our own true nature. This way of treating oneself and the world leads to a mechanical way of thinking, which is the cause of so much of our suffering. Zen aims at overthrowing this distorted view of the world, and zazen is the means of doing it.

On coming out of samadhi it can happen that one becomes fully aware of one's being in its pure form; that is, one experiences pure existence. This experience of the pure existence of one's being, associated with the recovery of pure consciousness in samadhi, leads us to the recognition of pure existence in the external world too.

To look at oneself and the objects of the external world in the context of pure existence is *kensho,* or realization. And this has been achieved, since Buddha himself did so, by men and women of every generation, who bear witness to its reality.

This experience is attained by the training of body and mind. Reason comes later and illuminates the experience.

IF YOU GO CLIMBING IN THE MOUNTAINS, you were probably led to do so in the first place by the beauty of the mountains. When you start to climb, however, you find it is a matter of working one's way along patiently, step by step, progressing with great care and caution. Some knowledge of climbing technique is essential.

It is the same with Zen. We take it up in the search of the meaning of life, or in the hope of solving the problems of our existence, but once we actually start, we find we have to look down at our feet, and we are faced with practice followed by more practice.

Our aim in practicing zazen is to enter the state of samadhi, in which, as we have said, the normal activity of our consciousness is stopped. This is not something that comes easily to us.

Beginners in Zen will usually be told to start by practicing counting their breaths — that is, to count each exhalation up to ten, and then start again.

Try this for yourself. You may think you can do it without difficulty, but when you start you will soon find that wandering thoughts come into your head, perhaps when you have reached about "five" or "six," and the thread of counting is broken. The next moment you come to yourself and can't remember where you left off. You have to start again, saying "one" and so on.

How can we prevent our thoughts from wandering? How can we learn to focus our attention on one thing? The answer is that we cannot do it with our brain alone; the brain cannot control its thoughts by itself. The power to control the activity of our mind comes from the body, and it depends critically (as we see later) on posture and breathing.

WITH REGARD TO POSTURE, we need only say at this stage that stillness of body engenders stillness of mind. Immobility is a first essential. Traditionally, and for good reasons, we sit down to practice, because (among other reasons) it is in this position that we can keep our body still but our minds wakeful.

Immobility results in a diminution of the stimuli reaching the brain, until eventually there are almost none. This gives rise, in due course, to a condition in which you cease to be aware of the position of your body. It is not a state of numbness, for you can move your limbs and body if you want. But if you keep your body still, it is not felt.

We call this condition "off-sensation." In this state the activity of the cortex of the brain becomes steadily less and less, and this is preliminary to entering samadhi.

We continue to breathe, of course, as we sit, and find that our ability to concentrate our attention, to remain wakeful, and ultimately to enter samadhi depends on our method of breathing.

Even those who have not practiced zazen know that it is possible to control the mind by manipulating the breathing. Quiet breathing brings about a quiet state of mind.

In zazen, we breathe almost entirely by means of our abdominal muscles and diaphragm. If the lower abdomen is allowed to fill out, the diaphragm is lowered, the thoracic cavity (between the neck and abdomen) is enlarged, and air is taken into the lungs. When the abdominal muscles contract, the diaphragm is pushed up, expelling air from the lungs.

The slow, sustained exhalation that we adopt in zazen is produced by keeping the diaphragm contracted so that it opposes the action of the abdominal muscles, which are trying to push air out of the lungs. This opposition generates a state of tension in the abdominal muscles, and the maintenance of this state of tension is of utmost importance in the practice of zazen.

All other parts of the body are motionless, and their muscles are either relaxed or in a state of constant, moderate tension. Only the abdominal muscles are active. As we explain later, this activity is a vital part of the mechanism by which concentration and wakefulness of the brain are maintained.

Traditionally, in the East, the lower part of the abdomen (called the *tanden*) has been regarded as the seat of human spiritual power. Correct zazen ensures that the weight of the body is concentrated there, producing a strong tension.

The essential point we want to make is that it is the correct manipulation of the lower abdomen, as we sit and breathe, that enables us to control the activity of our mind. Posture and breathing are a key to concentration, to stilling the activity of the mind, and to entering samadhi.

When we put it so briefly, our conclusions may seem far-fetched. If they do not seem convincing on the page, the reader should experiment for him- or herself along the lines we indicate. Zen is above all a matter of personal experience. Students are asked to accept nothing as the truth that they cannot demonstrate for themselves, with their own mind and body.

IN THE STATE OF "OFF-SENSATION," we lose the sense of the whereabouts of our body. Subsequently, by stilling the activity of the mind, a state is reached in which time, space, and causation, which constitute the framework of consciousness, drop away. We call this condition "body and mind fallen off."

In ordinary mental activity the cerebral cortex takes the major role, but in this state, it is hardly active at all. "Body and mind fallen off" may seem to be nothing but a condition of mere being, but this mere being is accompanied by a remarkable mental power, which we may characterize as a condition of extreme wakefulness.

To those who have not experienced it, this description may seem strange, yet the condition really does occur in samadhi. At the time, however, we are not aware of it, because there is no reflecting activity of consciousness, and so it is hard to describe. If we try to describe it, however, it would be as an extraordinary mental stillness. In this stillness, or emptiness, the source of all kinds of activity is latent. It is this state that we call pure existence.

IF YOU CATCH HOLD OF THIS STATE OF PURE EXISTENCE, and then come back into the actual world of conscious activity, you will find that Being itself appears transformed. This is why Being is said to be "veiled in darkness" to the eyes of those who have not experienced pure existence. When mature in the practice of zazen, Being is seen with one's own eyes.

However, just as energy can be used for many different purposes, so can pure existence be experienced in relation to any phase of life — anger, hatred, or jealousy as well as love and beauty. Every human action must be carried on through the ego, which plays a role comparable to that of a pipe or channel through which energy is conducted for different uses. We usually think of the ego as a kind of constant, unchanging entity. In fact, however, it is simply a succession of physical and mental events or pressures that appear momentarily and as quickly pass away.

So long as our mind operates subjectively, however, there must be a subject that functions as the ego. As there is normally no cessation of subjective activity, there can normally be no state in which we are devoid of an ego. However, the nature of this ego can change. Every time we succeed in banishing a mean or restricted ego — a petty ego — another ego with a broader outlook appears in its place, and eventually what we may call an "egoless ego" makes its appearance.

When you have acquired an egoless ego, there is no hatred, no jealousy, no fear; you experience a state in which you see everything in its true aspect. In this state you cling to or adhere to nothing. It is not that you are without desires, but that while desiring and adhering to things you are at the same time unattached to them.

The Diamond Sutra says, "Abiding nowhere, let the mind work." This means: Do not let your mind be bound by your desire, and let your desire occur in your mind. True freedom is freedom from your own desires.

When you have once experienced pure existence, you undergo a complete about-face in your view of the world. But unfortunately, as long as we are human beings, we cannot escape from the inevitability of living as individuals. We cannot leave the world of differentiation. And so we are placed in a new dilemma, one that we did not encounter before. Inevitably, this involves a certain internal conflict, and may cause much distress. To deal with this, further training of the mind has to be undertaken to learn how, while living in the world of differentiation, we can avoid discrimination.

We have to learn how to exercise the mind of nonattachment while working in attachment. This is called training after the attainment of realization, or cultivation of Holy Buddhahood, which constitutes an essential part of Zen.

There is a Zen saying, "Differentiation without equality is bad differentiation; equality without differentiation is bad equality." This is a common saying, but the level of understanding it refers to is not common, since it can be attained only in a mature state of Zen practice.

ZEN TRAINING CONTINUES ENDLESSLY. The mean or petty ego, which was thought to have been disposed of, is found once again to be secretly creeping back into one's mind. Long, chronic habits of consciousness are so firmly implanted in our minds that they haunt us perpetually, and it is impossible for us to inhibit them before they appear.

The longer we train ourselves, however, the more we are liberated from the petty ego. When the petty ego appears, do not be concerned with it. Simply ignore it. When a negative thought strikes you, acknowledge it, then drop it.

The Zen saying goes, "The occurrence of an evil thought is an affliction; not to continue it is the remedy."

ZEN TALKS ABOUT "EMPTINESS." What is meant by this?

When a thought appears in your mind, it is necessarily accompanied by internal pressure. Emptiness is a condition in which internal mental pressure is totally dissolved.

Even when you think, "It's fine today," a certain internal pressure is generated in your mind, and you feel you want to speak to someone else and say, "It's fine today, isn't it?" By doing this, you discharge the pressure.

In Zen texts the word *mushin* occurs. Literally, this means "no mind" (*mu,* no; *shin,* mind), which means "no ego." It means the mind is in a state of equilibrium.

We think every moment, and an internal pressure is generated, and we lose equilibrium. In Zen we train ourselves to recover equilibrium every moment. The ego is built up from a succession of internal pressures. When the pressures are dissolved, the ego vanishes, and there is true emptiness.

A student of Christianity, hearing that Zen talks of emptiness, offered for comparison a definition of holiness. Holiness, he said, means completeness, with nothing added to it.

The word holiness is found in Buddhism, too. A Buddha is holy. But in Buddhism, when you become a Buddha, you are supposed to forget you are a Buddha. When you are conscious of being a

Buddha, you are not truly a Buddha, because you are ensnared by the idea. You are not empty. Every time that you think you are achieving something — becoming a Buddha, attaining holiness, even emptiness — you must cast it away.

IN A FAMOUS ZEN EPISODE, Joshu asked his teacher Nansen, "What is the way?"

"Ordinary mind is the way," was Nansen's answer.

But how can we attain this ordinary mind? We could say, empty your mind, and there is ordinary mind. But this is to resort to exhortation, or to a merely verbal explanation of what Zen aims at.

Students of Zen must realize it for themselves.

CHAPTER TWO

Zazen

Posture

WHEN DOING ZAZEN, we normally sit on the floor, facing the wall, on a cushion or folded blanket about three feet square. Another cushion or pad, smaller and thicker, is placed under the buttocks (Fig. 5). It is important that this pad be thick enough, since otherwise it will be difficult to take up a correct, stable posture.

A number of different postures can be used in zazen, and students should experiment to discover which suits them best. Provided the student can maintain a stable, motionless position without discomfort for twenty to thirty minutes, it does not matter much what posture is adopted.

If it is not possible to sit comfortably on the floor, one may try sitting on a chair or stool, adopting the essential features of the postures described below as far as possible. Wear loose clothes that do not constrict any part of the body. Much patient practice and experiment may be necessary to learn how to sit well.

Figure 1 shows the full-lotus position. It is symmetrical, with the right foot on the left thigh and the left foot on the right thigh. The reverse position can also be adopted. In this, as in all other positions, both knees rest firmly on the cushion.

The hands rest in the lap, usually with the right hand under the left and the palms turned upward. The thumbs may touch at their tips, forming a circle, or they may rest parallel to the other fingers. An alternative hand position is to grasp the thumb of one hand in the palm of the other (Fig. 2). The full lotus is a difficult position for most people when they start their practice. It is a completely balanced, self-contained position, however, and most conducive to good practice.

FIG. 1 The full-lotus position.   FIG. 2 The half-lotus position.

A less difficult posture is the half-lotus position (Fig. 2). Here the right foot is under the left thigh and the left foot is on the right thigh. (Again, the reverse is also possible.) This is an asymmetrical posture and tends to pull the spine out of line, one of the shoulders being raised in compensation. It is possible to correct this with the aid of a mirror or another person, but it should be recognized that this position sometimes results in other defects in posture, notably certain slight distortions of the upper body. We cannot recommend this position very much. You might as well place the edge of one foot on the shin of the other leg. Then the style approaches that shown in Fig. 3 and can be recommended.

Figure 3 shows a modified Burmese style, with both feet flat on the cushion. Take care not to fall into the cross-legged position of the tailor, where the waist is lowered backward. The waist should always be pushed forward in the way that will be described below. This position is completely symmetrical and conducive to the relaxation of the upper body.

A different posture is shown in Figure 4, in which students straddle their pad, resting their weight on it and on their knees. This style is very effective, especially for beginners wishing to learn how to stress the lower abdomen correctly. If you adopt this position and push the waist forward, the stress will naturally be thrown into the bottom of the abdomen.

In all these positions the stable base for the body is a triangle formed by the buttocks and the two knees, and so it is important to find a posture where the knees rest firmly on the cushion and bear the weight of the body. The pelvis is held firmly fixed, and the trunk is placed squarely on it, not leaning in any direction.

The trunk is held upright by the waist muscles. These muscles are of great importance in bodily posture. They spread out widely, some penetrating deeply in the body, and their upper portions reach high into the upper regions of the back. In all postures it is these muscles that hold the trunk up straight, and it is these muscles alone that are particularly contracted.

It is important that, as far as possible, the body be kept perfectly upright when viewed from the front. It should be possible to draw a vertical line from the center of the forehead, nose, chin, throat, and navel, ultimately down to the coccyx (Fig. 6). Any deviation should be carefully corrected, not only in zazen but in one's ordinary carriage.

FIG. 3 A modified Burmese posture.

FIG. 4 A posture in which the legs are directed backward and placed on either side of the pad.

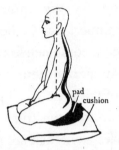

FIG. 5 The configuration of the spinal cord in a correct posture. Note that the spine is not held in a straight line.

FIG. 6 This figure illustrates the method of relaxing and lowering the shoulders by placing the hands on the legs and exhaling deeply. In a correct posture a vertical line can be drawn through the center of the forehead, nose, chin, throat, and navel.

FIG. 7 In a correct zazen posture the buttocks and knees form a triangle that acts as a base for the body. The weight of the body is concentrated in the lower abdomen, with the center of stress in the tanden (T). The trunk is perfectly vertical.

ONCE YOU HAVE TAKEN UP any of the above positions, the next step is to make sure the waist and lower abdomen are correctly positioned. The essential movement here is to push the waist forward, and tip the top of the pelvis forward. This in turn pushes the lower abdomen forward and at the same time throws the buttocks backward.

The importance of pushing out the belly in zazen has long been advocated. When you hold your trunk up straight the weight of the body is necessarily concentrated in the lower abdomen, and the region a few inches below the navel is the center of the stress. This region is called the tanden (Fig. 7; note that in a more general sense this term is applied to the whole of the lower abdomen).

When the weight of the body is concentrated in the tanden, the most stable posture and the quietest mental condition are achieved. In zazen the lower abdomen should fill out naturally by the combined action of the forward movement of the waist and the funneling of the weight of the body into this region.

Viewed from the side, the spinal column is not a straight line but is gently curved, as illustrated in Figure 5. The position of the head and neck is of some importance. It is not a bad thing if the face is turned slightly downward, just as some images of the Buddha look down, with the forehead very slightly stuck out and the chin drawn in a little. Keeping the neck slightly slanted forward and quite motionless helps you to get into samadhi; you may find yourself doing this involuntarily as your practice develops and you approach samadhi. If you prefer, however, you may simply hold your head and neck upright.

The body as a whole must be quite motionless, since this is a necessary condition for entering samadhi.

Finally, the chest and the shoulders should be relaxed and lowered. By doing this, tension in the shoulders, neck, and the pit of the stomach will be relieved. Place your hands on your knees, with the knuckles forward, and exhale deeply. This is not the formal position of the hands in zazen, but you will quickly discover in this way how to lower the chest and shoulders and thereafter do it routinely. The movement of the buttocks backward also pulls down certain muscles in the shoulders and helps to release stress in the chest and shoulders.

WITH THE CORRECT POSTURE, zazen becomes completely comfortable. Faulty postures can make zazen highly uncomfortable. It is important that the trunk is placed squarely on the pelvis. Students should not lean their heads, spine, or trunk to the left or right. By sitting before a mirror, stripped to the waist, you can see where you are out of alignment by carefully examining your posture and moving the body into various positions to find out which part of the body must be relaxed and which parts tensed.

I used to experience a dull pain in one of my buttocks after sitting for a long time. I assumed it was inevitable and never thought to ask myself the reason. But the fact was that my body was slightly inclined so that my weight was thrown more on one side than the other. It took me a long time to understand such a simple thing.

Most of us know very little about our posture and we maintain quite faulty habits, both in zazen and in ordinary activities. When you take up a correct posture you find that not only the shoulders but the muscles of the back, the sides, and other quite unexpected parts of the body are relieved of strain.

When one takes up a correct posture the weight of the body is concentrated directly in the tanden. A strong internal pressure is produced there that is important for controlling the mind and entering samadhi.

Now, it is true that partial distortion of the spinal column is found in many people. If inborn, or acquired very young, one's settled constitution has to be regarded as semipermanent — and it may be a mistake to try always to impose the "correct" posture. Some may well be comfortable with accustomed postures, and they should continue with those postures. A slight deviation from the standard does not prevent them from getting into samadhi.

You can get into samadhi even sitting in an easy chair in a casual posture, and there are many examples of sick people, confined to bed, who have attained maturity in Zen.

For most of us, however, it helps greatly if we follow as closely as possible the general principles of correct posture that I have described here. A mature Zen student has only to sit down to enter almost immediately into samadhi. It is an outcome of correct posture.

CHAPTER THREE

Breathing in

Zazen

ONE-MINUTE ZAZEN

Let's try an experiment that we call "One-Minute Zazen":

With your eyes wide open, stare at something in the distance: the corner of the building outside the window, a point on a hill, a tree or a bush, or even a picture on the wall.

At the same time stop, or nearly stop, breathing, and with your attention concentrated on that one point, try to prevent ideas from coming into your mind.

You will find that you really are able to inhibit thoughts from starting. You may feel the beginnings of some thoughtlike action stirring in your mind, but that, too, can be kept under control.

Repeated practice will give you the power to inhibit the appearance of even the faintest shadow of thought.

This inhibition can be sustained as long as the breath is stopped or almost stopped. Your eyes are reflecting the images of outside objects clearly, but "perception" does not occur. No thinking of the hill, no idea of the building or picture, no mental process concerning things inside or outside your mind will appear. Your eyes simply reflect the images of outside objects as a mirror reflects them. This simplest mental action may be called "pure sensation."

William James, in his classic *Textbook of Psychology,* depicts this pure sensation as follows:

"Sensation distinguished from perception — It is impossible rigorously to define a sensation ... and perceptions merge into each other by insensible degrees. All we can say is that *what we mean by sensations are first things in the way of consciousness.* They are the *immediate* results upon consciousness of nerve-currents as they enter the brain, before they have awakened any suggestions or associations with past experience: absolutely pure sensation.

"The next impression produces a cerebral reaction in which the awakened vestige of the last impression plays its part. Another sort of feeling and a higher grade of cognition are the consequence. 'Ideas' *about* the object mingle with awareness of its mere sensible presence, we name it, class it, compare it, make propositions concerning it. ... In general, this higher consciousness about things is called *perception,* the mere inarticulate feeling of their presence is called sensation. We seem to be able to lapse into this inarticulate feeling at moments when our attention is entirely dispersed."[1]

In our experiment of One-Minute Zazen, sensation resulted from strong inhibition of the process of thinking. While James considered that to some degree we seem able to "lapse into this inarticulate feeling at moments when our attention is entirely dispersed," in our One-Minute Zazen strong mental power controls our mind and inhibits dispersed attention and wandering thoughts. It is not an inarticulate state of mind but a strong, voluntary, inward concentration.

Where does this mental power come from? In our experiment it came from stopping (or almost stopping) breathing. And stopping breathing necessarily involves straining the abdominal respiratory muscles — in other words, developing tension in the tanden.

Mental power, or we might say spiritual power, in the sense of this strong inward concentration, comes from tension in the tanden. At first this may sound somewhat ridiculous. But it proves true, as we shall try to show.

Try the following:

Sit down quietly for a time with the intention of not thinking anything.

Presently, however, some idea will come into your head, and you will become absorbed in it and forgetful of yourself. But before long you will suddenly become aware of yourself and start once again trying not to think anything.

Before perhaps twenty seconds have passed, however, you will once again find a new idea cropping up and will be drawn into thinking about it, forgetful of yourself. Repeat the same process time and time again, and at last you come to realize that you cannot control the thoughts occurring in your own mind.

Now try a variation of the One-Minute Zazen exercise:

Stop, or nearly stop, your breathing. Then breathe slowly and deeply, repeatedly generating new tension in the abdominal respiratory muscles. You will find your attention can be sustained by the tension of the respiratory muscles.

Breathing has an extremely important role in controlling thoughts in zazen practice. When you observe carefully how it is done, you find a tremendous amount of effort is being used. Even in spite of this, certain lapses of concentration appear and thoughts threaten to creep in. Each time, they can be inhibited by a renewed effort of concentration.

The effort involves keeping up or renewing the tension in the respiratory muscles. This tension leads to samadhi, which is a steady wakefulness, with thoughts controlled and spiritual power maximally exerted.[2]

THE IMPORTANCE OF BREATHING IN ZAZEN

Let's consider some simple facts about the physiology of breathing and see how they apply to zazen. These are illustrated in Figure 8.[3]

Toward the bottom of the figure is a line at approximately the 1.2 liter level called *residual volume*. Even though all of the muscles of expiration are fully contracted, 1.2 liters of air still remain in the lungs, because no amount of muscular contraction can completely collapse all of the alveoli and respiratory passages. This is why in zazen we

can exhale as much air as possible and then remain
without breathing for a considerable period.

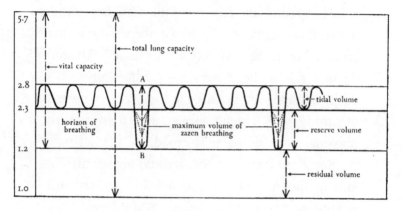

FIG. 8 Diagram illustrating the volume of air taken into and
expelled from the lungs in breathing. The thick, continuous line
shows the successive inhalations and exhalations in zazen. Deep
exhalation, in which all or most of the reserve volume is expelled,
is followed by a number of cycles of normal breathing.

The rising and falling curve between the levels
of 2.3 and 2.8 liters represents normal respiration.
The inflow and outflow of air with each respiration
is known as the *tidal volume.*

At the end of a normal expiration, if you contract all the respiratory muscles as powerfully as
possible, you can force approximately 1.1 liters of
additional air from the lungs. This extra air that can

be expired only with effort is known as the *expiratory reserve volume.*

The vertical line AB shows the maximal volume of breathing in zazen. When we make the maximal effort, all of the reserve volume is exhaled. We don't do this repeatedly, however — following such a deep expiration, some three to five cycles of normal breathing will usually follow, and then another maximal expiration is performed.

Some students will not go so far toward the bottom of the reserve volume but will return from around midway or so, as shown by the dotted lines. If you do not go so far below the horizon, you will not need the tidal recovery breathing. The further you go below the horizon, however, the more quickly you will attain samadhi and the deeper it will be.

IN ZAZEN, the thoracic cage (between neck and abdomen) is to be kept as still as possible. Inhalation is done by inflating the lower abdomen, while exhalation is performed by contracting the abdominal muscles.

There is an important difference between normal

breathing and breathing in zazen: In zazen, the free contraction of the abdominal muscles and their upward pushing movement are opposed by the diaphragm. This produces bated breath.

This sounds complicated, but is in fact very simple: you have only to hold your breath. If you then expire slowly, little by little, it is necessarily done by holding the diaphragm down and steadily checking the upward pushing movement of the abdominal muscles. This is what we mean when we speak of "throwing strength into the tanden." It results in the generation of what ultimately proves to be spiritual power.

If you manage to keep the diaphragm and the abdominal muscles contracting in opposition with almost equal strength, your breath will almost be stopped, though there is some quiet and almost imperceptible escape of breath from the lungs because of the natural bodily pressure. When we speak of stopped, or almost stopped, breath, we generally mean the state of very quiet respiration.

At the beginning of this chapter we described the experiment of One-Minute Zazen and found we could control thoughts occurring in the brain by holding our breath. That control and inhibition of thought came from this opposed tension in the abdominal muscles and diaphragm. From the experience of zazen we are bound to conclude that by maintaining a state of tension in the abdominal respiratory muscles we can control what is happening in the brain.

Even those who know nothing about Zen will throw strength into the abdomen, by stopping their breath, when they try to put up with biting cold, bear pain, or suppress sorrow or anger. They use this method to generate what may be called spiritual power.

The abdominal muscles can be regarded as a kind of general manager of the muscular movements of the entire body. When doing heavy manual work, such as weight lifting or wielding a sledgehammer, you cannot bring the muscles of the rest of the body into play without contracting these muscles. Even in raising a hand or moving a leg you are using the abdominal muscles. Scribble with your pen or thread a needle and you will find tension developing in the diaphragm. Without cooperation of the respiratory muscles you cannot move any part of the body, pay close attention to anything, or, indeed, call forth any sort of mental action. We cannot repeat this fact too often: it is of the greatest importance but has been rather ignored up to now.

What is described in this chapter is not found elsewhere in Zen literature. It is a new proposal. Of course, if you are experienced in zazen and do not like the method proposed here, you may ignore it. However, as your practice develops you may come to see the value of it.

Counting and following the breath

It is usual to begin the practice of zazen by counting your breaths. There are three ways of doing this:

1. Count both inhalations and exhalations. As you inhale, count "one" inwardly; as you exhale, count "two," and so on up to ten. Then return to one again and repeat the process.

2. Count your exhalations only, from one to ten, and repeat. Let the inhalations pass without counting them.

3. Count your inhalations only, letting the exhalations pass without counting them.

Of these three, the first method is generally used for the initiation of beginners, the second is recognized as a more advanced step, and the third is somewhat difficult for a beginner but gives good training in inspiration.

When beginning to practice the first method, it may be helpful to whisper the count inaudibly, or even audibly. Then, except for occasions when you feel the need for audible counting, concentrate on the counting inwardly.

In practicing the second method, say "won-n-n" with a lengthened expiration, and after taking a breath say "two-oo-oo" with the next expiration. With each count the expiration will naturally go down below the horizon of breathing. Thereafter you keep on, saying "three-ee-ee," "four-r-r," and so on, up to ten.

But in the middle of counting, some other idea will suddenly come into your head, and you will find yourself involved with that thought for a while. However, you will soon return to yourself and take up the counting again — but now you discover you have forgotten where you left off and must go back to the beginning and start from one again.

All beginners who try this practice for the first

time experience this, and are surprised by their inability to control their thoughts. Some readers may find this hard to believe. Then they should try it for themselves and see how their minds wander. That's exactly what a Zen teacher wants them to be aware of, and the teacher will say, "Use this method for a while to train your mind."

The third method is training in breathing. The most important thing in this case is to inflate the lower abdomen and inhale. In the course of saying "one," generally the tidal volume will be filled. As you approach the end of the inhalation it will tend to become chest breathing and you will have to make an effort to keep up the abdominal breathing.

POSITIVE SAMADHI AND ABSOLUTE SAMADHI

Although we discuss samadhi in detail in the next chapter, we want at this stage to make a clear distinction between the two kinds of samadhi, since it is important to our practice of counting breaths.

There are two kinds of samadhi: *absolute samadhi* and *positive samadhi*. People generally associate the term samadhi with Nirvana, in which the activity of consciousness is almost stopped. But the samadhi reached in counting the breaths involves a very definite action of consciousness. This, then, is an active sort of samadhi, which we call positive samadhi, to distinguish it from the other kind, which we call absolute samadhi.

We do not call it "negative samadhi," because absolute samadhi constitutes the foundation of all Zen activities and also because it leads us to experience pure existence.

To date, these two kinds of samadhi have not been clearly distinguished, and confusion has resulted. Some traditions of Zen involve a large element of positive samadhi, while absolute samadhi is more important in others.[4] We suggest that the right course is to develop positive and absolute samadhi equally.

To enter the silence of absolute samadhi is to shake off what we call the habitual way of consciousness — in an old phrase, "topsy-turvy delusive thought." By doing so we purify body and mind.

Then, going out (or coming back) into the world of actual life and of the ordinary activity of consciousness, we enjoy positive samadhi and freedom of mind in the complicated situations of the world. This is real emancipation.

When we return to counting breaths, a useful analogy can be drawn with the state of mind necessary in driving a car. When driving you are obligated to exercise two kinds of attention. The first is sharply focused, directed upon a certain limited zone ahead of you. The second is quite the opposite and is diffused over a broad area; you are on the lookout for emergencies arising in any direction.

Similarly, in counting breaths, both sharply focused and diffused attention are required. We have to concentrate on reciting the numbers, while at the same time being alert not to miss their order. This may sound easy, but in fact, the more you concentrate on the individual breaths and counts, the more difficult it is to keep the attention widely diffused at the same time. To accomplish the two things at once requires vital effort.

One final word about counting the breaths: If, after making good progress in zazen, you return to this practice once more, you will find that it leads to the development of an extraordinarily brilliant condition of consciousness. But this is not to be expected in the zazen of beginners. Teachers, therefore, are usually satisfied if students can master just the elements of counting the breaths and will then pass them to another kind of practice.

The students may suppose that they have finished with this sort of discipline and they will not have to practice it again, but this is mistaken. Students practicing alone may also revert to counting the breaths from time to time, even though they have gone on to other kinds of exercises.

FOLLOWING THE BREATH

A certain understanding of Zen makes people vaguely seek after absolute samadhi, even though perhaps not consciously. When you practice counting the breaths, if you recognize that it is a training in *positive* samadhi, you will find it brilliantly illuminating. But this will come only when you have made considerable progress in your study of Zen.

When beginners have worked on breath counting for a while they will find, without knowing why, that the counting is something of an encumbrance to them. They will wish to practice a quiet form of meditation in which the activity of consciousness will be transcended. Then, very naturally, they turn to the practice of following the breath.

Instructions for following the breath are very simple:

Follow each inhalation and exhalation with concentrated attention. At the beginning of your exhalation, breathe out naturally, and then when you reach a point near the horizon of breathing, squeeze the respiratory muscles so as nearly to stop breathing.

The air remaining in the lungs will almost imperceptibly escape, little by little. At first this escape will be so slight that you may not notice it. But presently it will become noticeable, and as the exhalation goes below the horizon you will find that the air is being pushed out intermittently.

If you regulate the escape of air in a methodical manner you will advance more effectively toward samadhi. The longer the exhalation, the sooner you will be there.

A very long exhalation, however, must necessarily be followed by short, rather quick respirations, because of the oxygen deficiency that results. This more rapid respiration need not disturb samadhi, as long as you continue with abdominal breathing. If you find this irregular method of breathing uncomfortable, try shorter exhalations.

WANDERING THOUGHTS

When using short or moderate exhalations, however, even those who have made considerable progress in zazen will often find it difficult to control wandering thoughts. Let us consider these wandering thoughts for a moment.

They are of two kinds. The first type is that which appears momentarily and disappears quickly. The second is of a narrative nature and makes up a story. The first type may be subdivided into two: (1) noticing someone coughing, the window rattling, birds chirping, and similar distractions that intrude momentarily from outside; and (2) the momentary thought that springs up from within, so that we think, "Now I am getting into samadhi," or "I am not doing well today." This sort of thinking does not disturb our getting into samadhi very much, and as samadhi progresses, these thoughts gradually disappear of themselves.

The second type of wandering thought is the sort of narration that occurs in daydreaming, in which you think, for example, of a recent conversation, and you are once again absorbed in the situation. While the body is apparently sitting in meditation, the mind is getting angry or bursting into laughter. These kinds of thoughts often happen when you are practicing moderate exhalations, and they are quite a nuisance.

Every so often you come back to yourself, notice the wandering thoughts, and pluck up concentration to control the fantasy. But eventually you find that your power is too weak. How can you get out of this condition?

There is no way other than by generating tension in the respiratory muscles by stopping or almost stopping the breath with a long, slow exhalation. That strength and energy give you the power to control wandering thoughts.

After a few long exhalations, you will find your

lower abdomen equipped with a strength you have never experienced in your ordinary breathing. It gives you the feeling, we might say, that you are sitting on the throne of existence.

This will naturally lead you to samadhi.

CHAPTER FOUR

Samadhi

Samadhi is the cleansing of consciousness,
and when consciousness is purified,
emancipation is, in fact, already accomplished.

THE FOUR CONDITIONS OF MIND

We have already seen a distinction between the two types of samadhi — absolute and positive samadhi. There are also several different phases of samadhi. To understand these phases, let's look at the way Rinzai Zenji, a great teacher of

Zen, categorized the conditions of mind. He taught that there are four conditions or states of mind, and each has its own phase of samadhi:

1. Inward concern is absent; outer concern dominates.

2. Outer concern is absent; inward concern dominates.

3. Both inner and outer concerns are absent.

4. Neither inner nor outer concerns are absent.

In the first condition, we are absorbed in outer circumstances. A famous surgeon was once performing a delicate operation when there was a sudden earthquake. The shocks were so severe that most of the attendants ran out of the room for safety, but the surgeon was so absorbed in the operation that he didn't feel the shocks at all. After the operation, he was told of the earthquake, and that was the first he knew of it. He had been completely absorbed in his work, in a kind of samadhi.

We experience this kind of samadhi when we are watching a football game, reading, writing, fishing, looking at pictures, talking about the weather, even stretching out a hand to open the door, even in the moment of sitting down or stepping forward — even in thinking. In fact, we are at every moment absorbed in that moment's action or thought.

There are various degrees of absorption, various periods of time, and differences between voluntary and involuntary attention. But we are almost always experiencing a minor or major condition of momentary samadhi, so to speak.

When we are in this sort of samadhi we are forgetful of ourselves. We are not self-conscious about our behavior, emotions, or thought. The inner person is forgotten and outer circumstances occupy our whole attention.

To put it another way: Consciousness works in two different ways, one directed outward, the other inward. When consciousness is concerned with outward matters, inward attention is forgotten, and vice versa.

NOW, IT IS IMPORTANT TO RECOGNIZE the difference between true samadhi with self-mastery (more on this soon) and the false kind of samadhi without it.

In true samadhi, even when your inner experience is forgotten, it is not forsaken. When you practice zazen, you become firmly established within; you could say your inner experience is ready to express itself at any time.

False samadhi lacks this self-mastery from the outset. There can be fighting samadhi, stealing samadhi, hating samadhi, jealousy samadhi, worrying, dreading, upsetting samadhi, but all without the guidance of self-mastery. None of these are true samadhi as it is understood in Zen.

An animal or bird enjoys samadhi every moment. When it grazes in a meadow it is in a grazing samadhi. When it flies up at the sound of a rifle, it is in a flying samadhi. Mellowed by the evening sun, standing quietly for a long time motionless in the meadow, it is in what we might call a "mellowing samadhi" — a beautiful picture and a condition to be envied even by a human being.

The animal has no self-consciousness, however. Though much to be admired, the animal's samadhi is after all an animal samadhi, a lower state than humans are capable of. The mellow condition attained by some under the influence of drugs (LSD, for example) can be compared to that of animal samadhi. It is a regression to the primitive life.

When we don't lose self-mastery but are at the same time involved in external circumstances, we are in positive samadhi. The inner state is not forgotten, it is simply inactive.

THE SECOND CONDITION OF MIND indicates inner attention. When we practice meditation, we concentrate inwardly and there develops a samadhi in which a self-ruling spiritual power dominates the mind. This spiritual power is the ultimate thing that we can reach in the innermost part of our existence. We do not think about it, because subjectivity does not reflect itself, just as the eye does not see itself, but we are this ultimate thing itself. It contains in itself all sources of emotion and reasoning power, and it is a fact we directly realize in ourselves.

When this inner awareness rules within us in profound samadhi, circumstances are forgotten. No outward concern appears. This inward samadhi is what is called absolute samadhi, and it forms the foundation of all zazen practice. It contrasts with the positive samadhi of the first category. Positive samadhi is outwardly directed, in the world of conscious activity. Absolute samadhi is a samadhi that transcends consciousness.

When we simply use the term samadhi by itself we are generally referring to this absolute samadhi.

IN THE THIRD CONDITION OF MIND, both inner and outer concerns are absent. A discussion of this must include an explanation of self-consciousness. We have seen that consciousness functions in two ways, outwardly and inwardly. There is another important action exercised by consciousness: one that reflects upon its own thought.

This kind of reflection must be distinguished from general introspection, which deals with character or behavior. When we think, "It is fine today," we are noting the weather, but we are not noting that we are thinking about the weather. The thought about the weather may last only a fraction of a second, and unless our next action of consciousness reflects upon it and recognizes it, our thought about the weather passes away unnoticed. Self-consciousness appears when you notice the

thought that has just appeared, and you then recognize the thought as your own.

If we don't perform this noticing action, we
don't become aware of our thinking, and we will
never know that we have been conscious at all. We
may call this action of noticing our own thoughts
"the reflecting action of consciousness," to distinguish it from general introspection. I take some
trouble to identify this reflecting action of consciousness because, as we will see, it plays an important role in zazen.

Now, when one is in absolute samadhi in its
most profound phase, no reflecting action of consciousness appears. This is the third category when
both inner and outer concerns are absent. In a
more shallow phase of samadhi, a reflecting action
of consciousness occasionally breaks in and makes
us aware of our samadhi. Such reflection comes
and goes momentarily, and each time momentarily
interrupts the samadhi to a slight degree.

The deeper samadhi becomes, the less frequent
becomes the appearance of the reflecting action of
consciousness. Ultimately the time comes when no
reflection appears at all.

This state of mind is called "nothing." But it is

not vacant emptiness. It is the purest condition of our existence. It is not reflected, and nothing is directly known of it. Both inner and outer concerns are absent.

The great master Hakuin Zenji called this "the Great Death." The experience of this Great Death is not common in the ordinary practice of zazen among most Zen students. Nevertheless, if you want to attain genuine enlightenment and emancipation, you must go completely through this condition, because enlightenment can be achieved only after once shaking off our old habitual way of consciousness.

WHAT IS THE DIFFERENCE between sleep and samadhi? Samadhi never loses its wakefulness. It never loses its independence and freedom. It involves self-mastery and spiritual power, and it contains within itself all sources of emotion and intellect.

When you come out of absolute samadhi, you find yourself full of peace and serenity, equipped with strong mental power and dignity. You are intellectually alert and clear, emotionally pure and sensitive. You have the exalted condition of a great artist. You can appreciate music, art, and the beauties of nature with greatly increased understanding and delight.

It may be, therefore, that the sound of a stone striking a bamboo trunk, or the sight of blossoms, makes a vivid impression, and you experience the wonderful moment of realization we call *kensho*.[5] In this moment, you seem to see and hear beautiful things, but the truth is that you yourself have become beautiful and exalted. Kensho is the recognition of your own purified mind.

THE FOURTH CONDITION OF MIND, when neither inner nor outer concerns are absent, is attained in Zen students' maturity, when you go out into the world of routine and let your mind work with no hindrance, never losing the awareness you have established in absolute samadhi. If we accept there is an object in Zen practice, then it is this freedom of mind in actual living.

To put it another way: When you are mature in practicing absolute samadhi, returning to ordinary daily life you spontaneously combine in yourself the first and third conditions of mind. You are active in positive samadhi and at the same time firmly rooted, with self-mastery, in absolute samadhi.

This is the highest condition of Zen maturity. True positive samadhi achieved through Zen practice ultimately resolves itself into this fourth category.

You may practice zazen and make certain progress in absolute samadhi and be successful in establishing awareness within yourself. Then a new problem arises: How can you exercise this awareness in your actual life in the busy world? When sitting on a cushion doing zazen you can attain samadhi and experience that awareness, and realize that awareness is really your absolute self. But when you come out into your daily routine and eat, talk, and become active in business, you often find you have lost that inner awareness. You wonder how you can manage to maintain that inner awareness — described above in the second condition of mind — in your daily life.

You may return to the state of the first condition of mind and try to be absorbed in outward circumstances. But this, too, you find is very difficult. While sweeping, you cannot become sweeping itself. You are unable to forget all other things besides sweeping, as the surgeon was absorbed in his operation.

Of course, when you see a football game you become absorbed in it. But this is a passive, involuntary attention — anyone can be excited and shout, forgetting all other things, including our inner awareness. There can be absorption in fighting, or in dissipation, or in making love — all with inner awareness forsaken. Without this awareness, we can become victims at the mercy of outer circumstances.

This is a false or superficial samadhi. The samadhi of the first condition of mind is not this sort of thing. The missing ingredient is inner control, self-mastery. Although inner realization is not on the main stage of our samadhi, we are still wakeful inside.

In short, students who are puzzled how to retain our inner awareness in our daily lives are striving for the condition in which both the inner person and the outer concerns are not absent but are freely in action. In the first category our inner awareness was inactive; in the fourth category it has returned to the front line.

One who has attained maturity in Zen can

behave freely and not violate the sacred law: both inner awareness and outer circumstances are in vigorous activity and there is no hindrance. Only maturity in Zen will secure this condition — the ultimate aim of Zen practice.

CHAPTER FIVE

Pure

$\mathcal{E}$xistence

*The unprecedented experience came to him
suddenly, striking him like a thunderbolt,
and his every problem was solved in an instant.*

WE HAVE SPOKEN RATHER EASILY in this book of the zero level of consciousness, though it is admittedly no easy matter for the beginner to reach this state. There, exhalation is almost stopped, and after a long silence a faint breath stealthily escapes, and then a slight inhalation occurs. Here we encounter the purest form of existence.

Traditionally it is called Original Nature or Buddha Nature. It is the hushed silence of the snow-clad Himalayas. Or it can be likened to the eternal silence of the fathomless depths of the sea.

There is a koan that runs, *"Pick up the silent rock from the depths of the sea and, without getting your sleeves wet, bring it up to me."*

The silent rock is yourself. You are asked to pick yourself up from the depths of the sea. But first you will have to find yourself at the bottom of the sea, where eternal silence reigns, with no time, space, or causation and no difference between yourself and others.

EXISTENCE IN ITS PURE FORM

"Isn't such a state of being all but death?" you may ask. "Like the state of a patient in critical condition, or like an idiot who has human form but not human faculties?" No, not at all! The condition of being all but dead that occurs in the depths of samadhi is a great thing. There you can discover your true nature.

The activity of consciousness, contrary to expectation, conceals the real nature of existence and represents it in a distorted way. First you have to go through absolute samadhi, where the activity of consciousness is reduced to zero level, and where you can vividly see existence in its nakedness. After experiencing this, you once again come back into the world of the ordinary activity of consciousness, and at that moment, consciousness will be found to be brilliantly illuminating. This is positive samadhi.

There is a line in the sutras, *"The lotus flower in the midst of the flames."* Imagine a living lotus flower, with petals like diamonds, emitting the serene light of Nirvana in the midst of incandescent flames.

You can never experience this brilliant state of consciousness until the delusive way of thinking has fallen off in absolute samadhi.

The existence of an animal may seem to be mere living. The plant may live in the same way, at a more primitive level. Yet look at the flowers, with their individual beauty, color, and form. Or see the graceful feathers of the bird, or the splendid color and design on the back of the insect now perching on the rail of the porch. Such colors and designs cannot be found in the most highly developed human art. The flexible, elegant limbs of an animal, the cells of the organisms we see under a microscope, the crystal structure of minerals — all these exquisite formations make us stare in wonder: what made them as they are?

To say their beauty is simply the product of our thought is ludicrous. The flower is beautiful and cannot be otherwise. We appreciate it and cannot fail to do so. A child produces a masterpiece and the adult cannot help admiring it. This is because existence itself is beautiful, and those who look at its forms are moved by their beauty.

We have identified consciousness as the eye of existence. It is deluded only because it is overcast. In absolute samadhi, existence manifests itself in its purest form; in positive samadhi, it displays itself in full bloom.

There is a poem in the *Hekigan Roku*, the classic Zen book of koans:[6]

Spring has come round.
A thousand flowers are in their lovely bloom.
For what? For whom?

Among the deep mountains and steep ravines, flowers come out unknown to us, and pass away unnoticed. Existence does not exist for others. It is of itself, for itself, by itself.

The beauty of nature is the manifestation of existence itself.

EXISTENCE AND CONSCIOUSNESS

The blind pushing on of existence, which wanted to recognize itself without being aware of this desire, proved successful when it created human consciousness and thereby obtained its own eye with which to examine itself. Human existence has succeeded in becoming conscious of its own beauty. To this extent it has raised itself to a higher level than can be found in the animal world or in the plant and mineral worlds. This level is rising continuously, and new beauty is now consciously created. This is intentional evolution.

As consciousness develops, however, its problems also become complicated. Not only beauty, but also diseases that have no parallel in the animal kingdom make their appearance in human life:

neuroses, schizophrenia, murder, rage, despair. But existence will never collapse. We cannot imagine that what conquered seemingly insurmountable obstacles in the past will ever be frustrated in the future.

Some deplore the present state of the world, regarding the world as being in decline or disintegration, and truly the "global village" may be facing disaster. People of earlier villages were totally annihilated, as in the Great Flood or the ruin of Sodom — and worlds, even solar systems and galaxies, have been pulverized in earlier eons, as the rings of Saturn, the asteroid belt, and cosmic dust in the Milky Way indicate.

While so many people earnestly pursue the cause of domestic and international harmony, and while so many others work to achieve national security and wealth, existence simply pushes on and on. It may be deluded, it may become awakened. Crises and despair are simply phases.

There is a saying, "Time and the hour run through the roughest day." That it cannot but exist has made existence pass through all sorts of emergencies, and has led to what it is. It must surely pursue the same course in the future.

DISEASES OF THE MIND

Those who are afflicted with mental troubles often do not realize that they are suffering from illness. In fact, almost all people are suffering from nervous disorders, and almost all people think of the mind as naturally that way. They never think of a remedy, since they are not aware of the disorder.

Literature is the mirror of the human mind. All the sufferings that are described in books are the results of mental disorders, yet there is no sign that the characters in novels — or their authors — recognize this. Rushing to destruction, being driven by passion to the point of total ruin: all this is admired. Nevertheless, it is a fever of the mind.

People die of mental illnesses, just as they die of physical diseases. Physical diseases are attended by a monitor called the mind. In mental illnesses the monitors themselves are sick. They are deranged, and helplessly lead the way to ultimate destruction.

True freedom of mind consists in not being dragged on by your own mind. To be free in this way comprises true freedom of mind and enables us to exercise genuine free will. Our environment, whatever it may be, is a mere accompaniment. We can achieve true freedom of mind regardless of the environment around us.

SINCE HAMLET SAID, "To be, or not to be — that is the question," or rather, since humans first appeared on earth, we have questioned the meaning of life. "Where did I come from, and where am I going? What is this life in the world I've been given, without being consulted?" These questions have tormented young people and are a primary cause of their disaffection — all because the truth of existence is not recognized.

This being is one's own being. From itself it has sprung. A simple thing! But in order to realize it, one has once to meet pure existence in the depths of absolute samadhi.

Animals live their lives blindly; they entertain no doubts. Children, too, live their lives wholeheartedly, because they accept the positive nature of existence. Only the adults are uneasy, because they have consciousness, which never feels at ease until it has seen through the secret of its own existence.

To ask what is the meaning of life is to inquire about the aim of life — its objective, its purpose. But think, does the sun shine with an aim? Has the baby come into the world with an aim? Existence only exists. It is impossible for it to be otherwise. Life is for life's sake, art is for art's sake, love for love's sake. A mother loves her baby because she loves it.

The delusive nature of consciousness comes from the fact that it necessarily belongs to the individual ego and serves the ego's individual needs. It cannot go beyond this individuality; it cannot think apart from the individual ego. This blind attachment of consciousness to the individual ego brings about "topsy-turvy delusive thought," from which stem (1) the world of opposition between oneself and others, (2) the craving for a constant imperishable ego, (3) the unsuccessful groping for satisfied existence, (4) vain searching for the root of the ego, (5) a sense of life as being confusing, incomprehensible, alien, or even dreadful, and (6) eventual dejection and the pervading feeling of "thrownness" (to use a favorite term of Heidegger's): unease and dissatisfaction.[7]

The secret of all this bewilderment lies in the failure to grasp the secret of existence.

Each of us has our own world of individual ego set against the outer world. The world of A's ego is incorporated into B's outer environment, and vice versa. C contains A and B in C's environmental circle. It is the same with D, E, F, and all the rest. Each of us has our own world of ego and environment, different from that of all others.

Emotional conflict and opposition of views and interests are therefore unavoidable, and alienation results. This is inevitable as long as human existence is divided into individual beings. Even Buddha, the successive patriarchs, and all Zen teachers are not exceptions to this.

Mature Zen students, however, hold existence embodied in themselves, and through the cultivation of Buddhahood come to realize the vacancy of the individual ego. They maintain themselves apart from the world of opposition and bring about its ultimate collapse, while those who remain confined in the world of opposition necessarily discriminate between themselves and others, and between themselves and the world, in every thought and action.

DECENTRALIZATION

A baby understands the outer world only from its own situation, through its sensations. However, as it grows up and its intellect develops, it can, in imagination, place itself in other positions and observe things from different viewpoints. In other words, it can decentralize its imaginative perceptions.

As children continue to grow up, they also develop the faculty of coping psychologically with far more complicated matters. They become able, in imagination, to change the relationship of their ego to all kinds of different states of affairs. They decentralize their egocentric views, both emotionally and intellectually.

As we mature, we put ourselves in the place of others and feel their sufferings. We delight with others, and grieve with them. We can experience others' sufferings as our own. We can fuse our existence with that of others.

This ability appears quite early on, in our relationship with our mother and with the rest of our family, and it shows itself later on in our relationships with our lovers and spouses. In the highly developed mind, this fusion can be extended to relations with friends and even with strangers. Such spiritual understanding can be called a kind of humanism. It has only a weak foundation, however, if it lacks the perfect realization of existence. Zen takes this foundation to be the beginning of everything. All conduct is based on this foundation.

HABITUAL DELUSIVE CONSCIOUSNESS

Most of us are equipped with what we call the delusive way of consciousness. Decentralization is rare; most of us are centered completely within our own egos, making use of others and of everything else in the world in the "context of equipment," to use Heidegger's phrase.

For most of us, consciousness is the watchdog of an egocentric individual being, while Zen understands a being as it is, and not as equipment: mountains as mountains, rivers as rivers, the rose beautiful as a rose, the flower of the weed beautiful as the flower of a weed, an ugly duckling as an ugly duckling.

If only you can realize the existence in an ugly duckling, you will find the ugliness suddenly turns, to your surprise, into illuminating beauty. Zen finds brilliant exemplification of existence in criminals, derelicts, and all of the rest of us. It recognizes existence in the animal, the plant, the stone.

Zen declares that matter and mind are one. It accepts things as they are.

We find in the drawings of Zen masters many objects and appliances: the sickle, raincoat, bamboo hat, earthenware pots, tea utensils, and flower vases. These are not looked upon simply as implements for utilization. The usefulness of each article has the same quality as the mind of the person using it.

When the tea masters take up a tea bowl and touch it to their lips, the bowl is alive. If you look penetratingly into that tea bowl, what an illuminating world of existence you find!

THE WAY OF NANSEN

A monk traveled a long way to see Nansen and found him cutting grass by the roadside. He asked, "What is the way to Nansen?"

Nansen answered, "I bought this sickle for thirty cents."

The monk said, "I do not ask about the sickle, I ask the way to Nansen."

Nansen answered, "I use it in full enjoyment."

When this dialogue is presented by a teacher as

a *koan*, if there has been no preliminary discussion about equipment, even a Zen student of considerable maturity may be puzzled as to how to answer. In Zen, "subject" and "use" are important terms: the subjectivity of existence and the use of it. In this koan, this use will eventually be understood by the student.

But what is use, after all? Is it something in the context of equipment? No, never. It is quite a different idea. It is the demonstration of existence. Nansen employed the sickle in the context of such use.

A brief comment on this topic would be easy. The monk asked the way to Nansen. If the original text is rendered word for word it runs, "Nansen way," which permits two meanings: "the way to Nansen" and "the way of Nansen." A Zen question often confronts you with the dilemma of two meanings. Whether this monk was conscious of the dilemma, whether he asked Nansen knowing who he was, whether he was a mature Zen student or a novice, is not known, and there is no need to know.

What is important is Nansen's answer. Let us first deal with Nansen's last words, "I use it in full enjoyment." Of course he did not use it merely as equipment; it was also used in the context of the use of Zen. In other words, it was the use of Nansen himself. It was Nansen's way of daily life — namely, Buddha's way. When you use a sickle or a hammer or a broom, or when you light a candle before an image of Buddha, if you do it in positive samadhi, it is the use of Buddha Nature. Nansen is the outstanding Zen master who said, "Ordinary mind, that is the way."

In the Zen monastery, the monks and lay residents work every day, sweeping, washing, cleaning, raking fallen leaves, weeding, tilling, gathering firewood. They are often exhausted by heavy labor. But if you work in a state of positive samadhi, you experience a purification of both body and mind. If you cannot experience this purification, and you find the work to be forced labor, then "thrownness" appears.

> Morning, sickle in hand,
> Noonday, roaming the forest,
> Gathering and binding wood,
> Now the evening moon,
> Quietly shedding her light
> On the path I tread.

How one enjoys cutting wood, gathering and binding it, and carrying it on the shoulders, treading the quiet evening path, dimly lit by the crescent moon. How one enjoys every movement of one's body, just as children enjoy it as they play at keeping house.

"I bought this sickle for thirty cents." Nansen bought the sickle as a child buys a toy at a toy shop. An adult buys in the context of equipment. This context secretly creeps into the relationship between people under the influence of the delusive way of consciousness. Even in marriage or friendship, the context of equipment will often be found to appear. A distortion of existence arises as a result, from which stem all the difficulties and sufferings of our minds.

But "I use it in full enjoyment" solves the problem. In this samadhi, "thrownness" finds no root to spring up from. You must not understand Nansen's "use" in the context of the user and the used. It is simply that he is using it in full enjoyment. Babies and children use themselves in samadhi every moment and enjoy every moment of life. They are affirmative in every way. The animal is in an animal-like samadhi; the plant, a plant-like samadhi; the rock, a rocklike samadhi. We find splendid samadhi in the physical world. Gravitation is samadhi itself! Confronted with a giant magnet, we are forced to feel it. Human beings alone have lost sight of samadhi, and of purification as well.

Internal pressure is blind. It often falls into error. However, now that it has acquired an eye to see itself with, it has the ability to correct its faults. It attains the capacity for decentralization to an increasing extent with the development of its intellect. This is the first step toward the correction of the delusive way of consciousness.

We have developed humanism, as well as religious movements, aimed at the fusion of individuals into universal existence. However, as we have said, unless one's life is based firmly on a consciously confirmed recognition of existence, this decentralization is resting on an insecure foundation. The outcome is imperfect. Zen clearly recognizes pure existence and on this basis carries through a perfect decentralization.

THE DIRECT EXPERIENCE OF EXISTENCE

Zen students train themselves earnestly in the first place only for the purpose of experiencing existence. However, when this is achieved — when existence is known — the business has only begun. Only the first step has been taken. An infinitely long further path extends before us. Therefore it is said:

Do you want to see the golden-faced Buddha?
Through countless eons, he is ever on the way.[8]

Life is full of problems, culminating in the inescapable problem of death. Our problems are impossible to solve by mere speculation or reasoning, and so we undertake the practice of zazen, involving as it does many years of tears and sweat. No peace of mind can be obtained unless it is fought for and won with our own body and mind. If once our body and mind have fallen off in absolute samadhi, we are then simply emancipated from the spell of the problems of life and death.

Zen literature abounds in poetical or word-transcending expressions, which may appear to be rather remote from the kind of approach to Zen that we have advocated in this book. Such expressions have come into use because when one wants to demonstrate directly the true nature of existence, one finds that ordinary conceptual description is inadequate.

And then there appears what we could call "language samadhi," in which the poetical expression of one's samadhi is understood by those who can place themselves in the same samadhi. We are greatly helped by this language samadhi in reaching Zen secrets.

But in spite of this, we wish to say that it is our intense desire to give a clear and intellectually acceptable demonstration of what has been regarded as a word-transcending secret. We think that this can be done, at least to a certain extent, if we make the fullest use of the achievements of modern culture. It will require the cooperation of many scientists and thinkers, and above all, the appearance of Zen genius. Genius may be a rare natural gift, but if you confine yourself to a single topic, working with a broad mental perspective, and persist in it, you will find yourself a genius.

When consciousness has lost its root, it finds itself floating like a piece of driftwood. Thrownness comes from this rootlessness. Only when consciousness is awakened and firmly grasps its root can it stand securely by itself.

PURE COGNITION

Once Nansen was in a dialogue with a high government official named Rikko Taifu, who had studied with Nansen and reached an advanced understanding of Zen.

Rikko said to Nansen, "Your disciple understands Buddhism a little."

"How is it during the entire twenty-four hours?" asked Nansen.

"He goes about without even a shred of clothing," replied Rikko.

Nansen said, "That fellow is still staying outside the hall. He has not realized the Tao."

"He goes without even a shred of clothing" is now a well-known Zen saying, referring to one who has stripped off all worldly attachments and is rid of topsy-turvy delusive thought. He has nothing. Nansen, however, was not satisfied with Rikko's reply, and said, "That fellow is still staying outside the hall." A fellow outside the hall is one who has not yet been granted the privilege of attending the royal court — in other words, the fellow had not yet attained fully the true spirit of Zen.

"Without a shred of clothing" may have been a fresh and original phrase in Rikko's day. It is used to denote nothingness and emptiness. But if students remain there, thinking that is the ultimate, they fall far short of true Zen attainment. When taught in this way, Rikko must have nodded his head in assent to Nansen's words. Judging from other descriptions of his behavior, he must have attained that much understanding.

IN ANOTHER STORY from the *Hekigan Roku* (Case 40), Nansen is in another dialogue Rikko Taifu:

Rikko said, "Jo Hoshi said, 'Heaven and earth and I are of the same root. All things and I are of the same substance.' Isn't that fantastic!"[9]

Nansen pointed to a flower in the garden and said, "People of these days see this flower as though they were in a dream."

What does this story mean? In response to Rikko, Nansen said, in effect, "See this flower: it is said that Buddha sees Buddha Nature with his naked eyes. Can you see it?" Rikko was confident of his understanding, but when he looked at the flower he could not see Buddha Nature there, only a peony.

Then Nansen passed his judgment: "People of

these days see this flower as though they were in a dream." There was no denying the difference in ability; Rikko was obliged to bow to Nansen.

Zen texts are sparing of words and express only the essential point. The important point is that Nansen put Zen truth under Rikko's nose.

Nansen introduced here the problem of cognition. Perhaps this was one of the earliest occasions in the history of Zen in which this problem was taken up so specifically.

Setcho, the author of the *Hekigan Roku*, comments on this story in a beautiful verse:

> Hearing, seeing, touching, and knowing
>   are not one and one;
> Mountains and rivers should not be viewed
>   in the mirror.
> The frosty sky, the setting moon at midnight,
> With whom will the serene waters of the lake
>   reflect the shadows in the cold?

Hearing, seeing, touching represent the auditory, visual, tactile, and other senses; *knowing* means cognition. *Not one and one* means that sensation and cognition are not to be separated from each other. Cognition and the cognized object are not strangers to each other but are interrelated, which makes transcendental cognition possible.

Mountains and rivers represent the external world. *The mirror* represents your subjectivity.

The frosty sky, the setting moon at midnight expresses the serene and sublime situation in which external object and sensation meet in pure cognition.

The serene waters of the lake are your mind, which exercises pure cognition. *Reflect the shadows* means pure cognition. *In the cold* again expresses the serene and sublime state of the mind when it exercises pure cognition. The mind is as serene and silent as the frosty sky, the setting moon, and midnight are purely cold.

Mountains and rivers should not be viewed in the mirror means that you should not say, as the idealist does, that the external world is nothing but the projection of the subjective mirror of your mind, and that sensation cannot transcend itself to hit upon the external object. The truth is the opposite of this. In profound silence, deep in the middle of the night, the lake serenely reflects the frosty sky, the setting moon, rivers, trees, and grass. The cognition occurs solemnly and exclusively between you and the objects.

Cognition is accomplished through two processes: first, pure cognition; second, the recognition of pure cognition. In pure cognition, there is no subjectivity and no objectivity. Think of the moment your hand touches the cup: there is only the touch. The next moment you recognize that you felt the touch. A touch is first effected just through the interaction between the hand and the object, and at that moment, pure cognition takes place. The next moment, the pure cognition is recognized by the reflecting action of consciousness, and recognized cognition is completed.

Then there arise subjectivity and objectivity, and one says, "There is a cup on the table." But at the moment when pure cognition is still going on, there is no subjectivity and no objectivity, just a touch — with no saying that there is a cup on the table. Transcendental cognition occurs through this meeting, but it is not yet recognized consciously.

When Setcho says, "The frosty sky, the setting moon," he is speaking of pure cognition, where there are only the frosty sky and the setting moon; no subjectivity, no objectivity; no one can peep into that moment, not even those who are looking at the sky and moon themselves, performing this cognition, because there is no reflecting action of consciousness. The moment is as solemn and serene as the frosty sky and setting moon are cold and silent.

When this is realized, the fourth line becomes very clear: "With whom will the serene waters of the lake reflect the shadows in the cold?" No one can notice the reflection, not even the one who does the reflecting (the doer is the lake, and maybe Setcho, or you yourself), because subjectivity cannot recognize itself.

PURE COGNITION AND KENSHO

Consciousness acts in two ways: (1) it recognizes objects in the external world, and (2) it can also turn its attention inward. In the first case, it directly receives a stimulus from the external world and gives rise to first sensation and then to thought or intuitive thinking. Sensation sees colors, flowers, mountains, and rivers, while intuitive thinking observes that it is fine weather, or feels love, hatred, and so on toward other people.

In the second case, attention is turned inward and recollects the past activity of the self. In absolute samadhi, sensation, thought, and intuitive thinking stop, or almost stop, their activity, and pure cognition reigns over the whole domain of the mind.

After once attaining such a condition of mind and then emerging from it into the world of conscious activity, we experience for a certain period of time a condition in which sensation alone is operative, working intuitively as it always does. We receive stimuli from the external world without restriction. Stimuli rush in, in all their unlimited profusion, and produce powerful impressions as they strike the mind.

This is the experience of kensho, the strength of the impressions that bring before you the objects of the external world with fresh and inspiring originality. Everything is direct, fresh, impressive, and overwhelmingly abundant at the time of the kensho experience.

CHAPTER SIX

Stages in

Zen Training

*Zazen is a matter of training yourself to become
a Buddha; rather, to return to being a Buddha,
for you are one from the beginning.*

IN SEARCH OF THE MISSING OX

Let us discuss a classic of Zen literature: a tra-
ditional series of pictures called *In Search of the
Missing Ox.*

I. STARTING THE SEARCH FOR THE OX

In Buddhist literature, the ox is likened to one's own True Nature. To search for the ox is to investigate this True Nature. The first stage in the sequence is the starting of the investigation.

Consider young men or women on the threshold of their lives. In their imaginations they expect many things of their future, sometimes in a joyful mood, sometimes in a pensive one. But what may be in store for them in life is not known to them until it actually happens.

They probably do not know what they really want from life, but in their naiveté they may think that they should work for others, denying themselves, even at the cost of self-sacrifice. "I must grapple with something serious. I want to know how the world is constituted, what my role in it should be. What am I? What am I to expect of myself?"

So they may think. Then, perhaps, these young people will start studying, shall we say, the philosophy of economics, and when they think they understand the power structure of the modern world they may rush off into some sort of activity with the goal of righting the wrongs of society and civilization. Others will take up the study of literature, philosophy, psychology, medicine, and so on.

Whatever direction they take, however, they tend to find that an intricate traffic network has been set up there, which quite often leads into some sort of complicated maze. Working in a situation that they did not originally imagine, habituation sets in, and before they know what has happened their path in life has become fixed.

A feeling that something is missing will make some of them knock at the door of religion.

Zazen is a matter of training yourself to become a Buddha; rather, to return to being a Buddha, for you are one from the beginning.

Now imagine you are standing at the door of Zen in search of your true nature: you are at the stage of starting the search for the ox.

2. FINDING THE FOOTPRINTS

Practicing zazen and reading Zen literature, you have acquired a certain understanding of Zen, though you have not yet experienced kensho.

At the first stage, when you started your search, you may have doubted whether you could attain your objective by going in this direction, but now you are confident that if you follow this path you will eventually reach your destination.

3. CATCHING A GLIMPSE OF THE OX

At length you come across the ox. But you see only a glimpse of its tail and heels.

You have had a kensho-like experience, but if you are asked where you came from and where you are to go, you cannot give a clear answer.

There are varieties of kensho, and have been from the outset. Sakyamuni Buddha's satori was a matter of creating a new world.

Before his time, it was not even known whether there was such an event. The unprecedented experience came to him suddenly, striking him like a thunderbolt, and his every problem was solved in an instant.

If the Buddha had not already been far advanced, however, he could not have explored in such a creative way this region that had never before been visited by any human being. Before this experience, the Buddha had passed the seventh and eighth stages in his training and had reached the ninth, "Returning to the Source." His was the thoroughgoing kensho that is real enlightenment.

Since his time, there have been many Zen teachers who had already finished the whole course of their training before they had their kensho experience. For many of them it took fifteen or even twenty years before this happened.

Now in the third stage we have a situation analogous to that in which beginners in painting find their work admitted, by a lucky chance, to an exhibition of the highest class. The beginners' paintings may be excellent, but it doesn't prove their ability as artists. Everything depends on their future endeavors.

Modern Zen students are told at the outset that there is an event called kensho awaiting them, and when they cross the path of this third stage they naturally take it for the vista that the Buddha saw, for the first time, when he stood on the peak of Zen practice. They are scrambling up among the rocks and bushes, expecting to see this view, and at the first glimpse of it they cry, "That's it!"

Of course, what they see is not false, but there is a great difference between their experience and that of the Buddha in content, beauty, and perfection.

4. CATCHING THE OX

At this stage, your kensho has become confirmed. As you see in the picture, however, the ox is inclined to run away willfully, and you have to hold it back with all your might.

In fact, you are experienced enough now to understand the saying, "Heaven and earth and I are of the same root; all things and I are of the same source," but in your everyday life you cannot control your mind as you wish. Sometimes you burn with anger; sometimes you're possessed with greed, blinded by jealousy, and so on. Unworthy thoughts and ignoble actions occur as of old.

At times, you are exhausted by the struggle against your passions and desires, which seem uncontrollable. This is something you did not bargain for; in spite of having attained kensho you seem to be as mean-spirited as ever. Even kensho seems to be the cause of new afflictions: You want to behave in a certain way but find yourself doing just the opposite. Your head is in the air, but your body is lying at the foot of the cliff.

You cannot let go of the bridle, however, and try to keep the ox under control, even though it seems to be beyond you.

5. TAMING THE OX

After great struggles the ox has at last begun to be moderately tame.

This is the time when the trainer thinks that the

wild animal is broken in and can perhaps be taught to perform some tricks.

6. RIDING THE OX HOME

The ox is now tame and obedient. Even if you let go of the bridle, it walks quietly homeward, in the evening calm, with you sitting peacefully on its back.

7. OX LOST, YOU REMAIN

Now kensho, enlightenment, even Zen itself are forgotten. No matter what holy feeling or marvelous state of mind you may experience, the moment you start to concern yourself with it and become conscious of it, it starts to be a burden.

Let events happen as they may, and simply let them stream by. When things have happened, they have happened; when they have gone, they have gone. The moment you settle down to some fixed view of things, decay is already setting in. "Abiding nowhere, let your mind work."

The verse of the Transmission of the Dharma by Buddha Vipasyin, the first of the Past Seven Buddhas, says:

Vice and virtue,
Sin and blessing,
All is vanity;
Abide in nothing.

8. No ox, no you

At the previous stage, "Ox Lost, You Remain,"
you probably thought everything was finished. But
now another stage appears, in which both you and
ox are forgotten. There is a Zen verse:

Last night, two clay bulls fought each other,
Disappearing in the sea in the fighting,
And nothing is heard of them this morning.

The moment your ego appears, circumstances appear. Subjectivity and objectivity accompany each other. When your ego vanishes, circumstances vanish.

A thought appears like a wisp of cloud in a bright summer sky. It comes and fades away silently in the blazing noontide serenity, and all is quiet again.

This stage corresponds to Rinzai's "Both inner and outer concerns are absent" (see chapter 4).

9. RETURNING TO THE SOURCE

You have only to emerge from the state of "No Ox, No You" to find that you have simply returned to the source. Just a flick and you are in the warm spring sunshine, with flowers blooming, birds singing, and people picnicking on the grass.

If you look carefully, you find it is the same old world you saw yesterday. The hillsides are covered with cherry blossoms; the valleys are full of spring flowers. But each of the flowers has its own face and talks to you. The things you see, the sounds you hear are all Buddhas. The old habitual way of consciousness has fallen off, and you have returned to the Pure Land.

Before reaching this stage, you had to go through the stage of "No Ox, No You." First you penetrated to the inside of yourself. The skins of the onion were peeled off one by one until it was reduced to nothing. That is absolute samadhi. But now you have come out into positive samadhi, in which consciousness is active.

In this stage of "Returning to the Source," what is experienced is in some ways identical to what was experienced in the third stage of "Finding the Ox," but there is all the difference in the world in the degree of profundity.

There is a Zen saying, "Ever shuttling from beginning to end." Your attainment is deepened by repeatedly coming back to the start, to the state of the beginner, and then retracing the path you have progressed. In this way your maturity becomes unshakably firm.

10. IN TOWN WITH HELPING HANDS

You mingle with the world. The picture shows a potbellied, carefree man (perhaps the great master Osho) who is now beyond caring about his personal appearance. He goes barefoot. He shows his chest. He cares nothing about how he dresses. All this symbolizes his mental nakedness.

He is carrying a basket with things for the townsfolk; his only thought is to bring joy to others. And what is in the gourd he is carrying? Perhaps the wine of life.

STEPS IN ATTAINING SAMADHI

In the commentary above we have talked in general terms about how one attains maturity in Zen. Let us now change the viewpoint and look at the pictures of *In Search of the Missing Ox* as a series of steps in attaining samadhi.

1. **STARTING THE SEARCH** for the ox is the time when the beginner is first initiated into how to sit, and how to regulate the breath and the activity of the mind. At this stage, beginners are naive, compliant, and intensely impressionable. The sound of the teacher's bell rings absolutely pure and seems to penetrate deep into their heart, purifying it. Everything creates a strong impression. Even a slight movement of the hand or the taking of a step is done with gravity, and this is very important and precious, though they may not realize it. It is much superior to a poor, commonplace kensho.

The beginner's mindfulness should never be lost, all through your training. Many students unfortunately do lose it later on, substituting for it various "meritorious" achievements to which they often attach great importance. The Zen student is supposed to leave the meritorious region and enter a meritless one.

2. **IN FINDING THE FOOTPRINTS**, the second stage, your practice of zazen begins to get under way, and you find your mind beginning to become quieter. You find to your surprise that all this time your normal state of mind has been noisy and agitated, and you have been unaware of it. You begin to realize that you have been suffering from a vague uneasy feeling, the origin of which you could not pin down. Now that you sit in zazen you are largely freed from it. You realize that zazen may be a means of quieting a disturbed mind.

When you first start the apparently simple practice of counting the breath, you are puzzled to find it not at all an easy matter. But through earnest effort, you become able to keep your diffused mind more sharply focused and gradually start to bring order to the activity of your consciousness. You realize that another dimension of mind is at work. But you feel far from experiencing genuine kensho.

3. IN CATCHING A GLIMPSE OF THE OX you experience, though only occasionally, a kind of samadhi. But it is unstable and you lack assurance. Nevertheless, your teacher may take your hand and pull you up into the meditation hall, saying, "That's it, that's it."

Gradually you acquire a certain confidence, and your practice gets under way. There are instances of students who one day explode with genuine enlightenment. This is called sudden and direct satori or enlightenment, in which one undergoes an exhaustive and profound experience all at once, just as Sakyamuni Buddha did.

Compared with this sudden and direct enlightenment, the method of gradual, step-by-step advance (the "installment plan" method, we might call it) is termed "ladder Zen." Whether we go by the ladder or in one jump, everything depends on one's determination to reach the top.

4. IN CATCHING THE OX an experience something like the following will occur:

"How long a time has passed, he does not know. Suddenly he comes back to himself, and feels as if he were at the bottom of the fathom-less depths of the sea. All is silent. All is dark. Was he asleep? No, his mind is wide awake. An internal strength seems to be welling up within him. He feels as if clad in heavy armor. Is this what the Patriarchs called 'silver mountains and iron cliffs'? His mind is as still and solemn as the snowy ravines of the Himalayas. No joy. No grief. Whether it is night or day, he does not know."[10]

Someday you will have this kind of experience. And one day, when you emerge from it, rising from your seat, stepping across the doorsill, looking at the stones and trees in the garden, hearing some trifling sound, raising a cup to your lips or passing your fingers over a bowl, suddenly you will find heaven and earth come tumbling down.

A new vista will be revealed to you. Just as the ripe bean pod splits open at the lightest touch of your fingertips, so your internal pressure brings about a new dimensional development of the mental world.

A critic might say that this is a matter of autosuggestion. But in fact the habitual way of consciousness has dropped off and a new mode of cognition, independent of space, time, and causation, is now at work. You and the external objects of the world are now unified. It is true that they are located outside you, but you and they interpenetrate each other. There is no spatial resistance between you and them.

In your earliest days, your daily life was full of such a way of cognition. But as you grew up, the elaborate way of consciousness consolidated its habitual mode of operation and separated itself from the external world, constructing the world of differentiation and discrimination. But now that habitual way has dropped off, and you are suddenly awakened to a new world.

That is kensho. *Ken* means seeing into something; *sho* means one's true nature. You find your true nature within yourself, and at the same time in the external world.

5. ONCE THE OX WAS CAUGHT, you thought you had it for good. But it was not so. Though sometimes you can get into samadhi, at other times you cannot. Now stillness of body and mind seem to appear; now you cannot control wandering thoughts.

"It could not have been samadhi," you say.

There is no remedy but to try again and again. Last year's harvest is last year's; this year's must be earned by hard work. And so the struggle is renewed, over and over again.

6. IN RIDING THE OX HOME, we must once more discuss the process of entering samadhi. The skin and muscles are normally constantly changing their tension, and it is largely through this that the sensation of bodily existence is maintained. But in the immobile posture of zazen, little change in muscular tension occurs, and off-sensation develops.

The skin reacts sensitively to this novel experience. A thrill-like sensation that runs through the entire body is experienced. It is like a sort of musical vibration, delightful and delicate, accompanied by a peaceful state of mind and by a beautiful stream of emotion that seems to flow from the heart.

Then peace and stillness start to fill the whole body. Samadhi develops from the stillness. With long practice, however, the delightful bodily sensation does not often appear. One simply sits down, and immediately begins to enter samadhi.

What is really going on inside the body when samadhi, preceded by these phenomena, appears?

Certain chemical changes must be occurring in us. We know that the body is constantly producing all manner of chemical compounds. Perhaps samadhi results from the production of certain specific chemicals in the body.

We are much against the use of drugs, such as marijuana, in zazen practice, but we would not oppose the view that zazen training in some way modifies the student's metabolism so that certain chemical substances are produced that facilitate the advent of samadhi. The fact that such substances are internally generated is a source of strength; externally supplied drugs weaken us by making us dependent upon them.

Whatever the physiological basis of samadhi may be, at this stage of "Riding the Ox Home" the student has achieved maturity and enjoys the freedom of his body and mind.

7. OX LOST, YOU REMAIN. This is the stage of wakeful samadhi, whether positive samadhi or absolute. You pay no particular attention to breathing, posture, and so on. Even lying in bed you can enter absolute samadhi.

On the plane of the normal activity of consciousness, working, talking, even riding in a jolting bus, you do not lose your positive samadhi. Formerly you and samadhi were two — were separated. You attained samadhi with effort. You were working on a dual system. But now this is not so. You are dominating; the realm of the mind has been brought under your rule.

8. No ox, no you. We can distinguish a number of levels of consciousness:

(a) The uppermost, where thoughts and ideas come and go.

(b) A level that understands but does not form ideas.

(c) A level that is only aware.

(d) A level that simply reflects interior and exterior objects as a mirror does. Even in this stratum, traces of the reflecting action of consciousness will occasionally appear, flashing momentarily upon the scene of your mind.

(e) The deepest level, where not even the faintest reflecting action of consciousness penetrates. Here certain ever-changing vestiges of mood remain. They are a kind of memory of one's lifetime, and also of one's predecessors. They want to rise up to the surface of consciousness and give expression to themselves. Even if they are not allowed to, they do not fail, remotely but importantly, to affect the trend of the activity of consciousness.

In absolute samadhi, however, the brain's activity is reduced to a minimum and the muddy layers of ancient memory are thoroughly cleansed. The habitual way of consciousness is swept away. Both the reflecting and the reflected vanish. This condition is called "no-thought samadhi," which is the same as absolute samadhi.

9. RETURNING TO THE SOURCE. In the previous stage a thorough and decisive purification of consciousness was carried out, and the muddy deposits, accumulated through countless eons, were dredged away. Now, in the present stage, the activity of consciousness starts up once more, with this cleansed condition of mind. It is like putting a brush to a clean sheet of paper: every stroke comes out shining bright.

If you listen to music, it sounds unimaginably exquisite. It is a state of positive samadhi in which the condition of kensho has become permanent. What is said of the Buddha will be true of you: you find Buddha's face wherever you turn your eyes.

Until yesterday you took great pains to develop the solemn state of absolute samadhi and fiercely checked all activity of consciousness. Now you let consciousness gaily open into full bloom.

10. IN TOWN WITH HELPING HANDS, the world of antagonism has dissolved; the habitual way of consciousness has totally dropped away. You no longer dress for ceremony or to impress anyone. You go barefoot, with chest bare. Everything is welcome. Wandering thoughts? All right! This is the Buddha's great meditation in the busiest activity of consciousness. You enjoy perfect freedom of playful, positive samadhi.

THE PATHOS OF THINGS

What a shock we experienced when we were still quite little children, when we realized for the first time that we must pass away, one by one, alone and separately, leaving behind our loved ones — father, mother, brothers, sisters. Perhaps you can remember this critical moment in your childhood, when you first experienced this sense of the "pathos of things."

It is not improbable that you were thrown by it into a kind of neurosis for a while; you had sad, sorrowful feelings toward others, perhaps even toward plants and animals. What you unconsciously felt at this time was a loss of unity with others, a deprivation of love.

It is from this deprivation of love that the feeling of the pathos of things stems. On a stroll in the moonlight in the country, or even on a busy street corner, we feel a certain yearning for something we cannot quite catch hold of. We do not know what it is, but the feeling infiltrates our whole being.

The mysterious, misty veil of the moonlight reminds us of eternity and distant lands, and this in turn makes us sensitive to the mutability of our actual life and brings about the melancholy mood. The pathos of things is a kind of homesickness. It is a sorrowful expression of the love we have lost, a yearning for homeland, faces, things, even for living and nonliving beings and things in general. The sense of the pathos of things is often to be found at the bottom of our sense of beauty, particularly when it arises from the expression of love obstructed by something fateful in life.

Humans are sometimes defined as the only beings who hate others. As long as we are a being in the world, however, we live with other people, and we are inseparable from each other. We cannot help feeling that we lack something when we are deprived of the chance of loving others and of being loved by them.

When you once experience absolute samadhi, and your egocentric, illusory thought falls away, you invariably develop love toward others. Then, however, you find that you must go through the frustrations of actual life. How are we to escape from this dilemma, from this seemingly irreconcilable conflict between separateness, distinction, and hostility on the one hand, and love on the other? Is this dilemma human fate?

Eternal cultivation of Holy Buddhahood after enlightenment helps us to solve this problem. Many Zen stories show how this problem was solved by our predecessors. Constant practice and experience of absolute samadhi give you the vision that enables you to see Buddha Nature with your naked eyes. Compassion and love toward strangers appear spontaneously.

You understand Sakyamuni Buddha's exclamation on the occasion of his enlightenment: "All the beings in the universe are endowed with the virtue and wisdom of the Buddha." You experience yourself the feelings of others — their sorrow, delight, humor, their whole personality — just as if they were your own feelings. The more firmly your samadhi is established, the more steadily does the illusory way of thinking fall away, and the less often discriminatory thinking occurs.

A new system of cognition is formed within you.

ABSOLUTE SAMADHI — The state reached in meditation, in which "the activity of consciousness is stopped and we cease to be aware of time, space, and causation.... A state in which absolute silence and stillness reign, bathed in a pure, serene light."

DHARMA — Has many meanings. It is used here (in chapter 6) to mean the laws of the universe; the teaching of Buddha.

KENSHO — The marvelous moment of realization sometimes experienced when emerging from absolute samadhi. *Ken* means seeing into something; *sho* means one's true nature. "You seem to see and hear beautiful things," Katsuki Sekida writes in *Zen Training*, "but the truth is that you yourself have become beautiful and exalted. Kensho is the recognition of your own purified mind." He also writes later (p. 238), "When one attains kensho and the habitual way of consciousness falls off, there appears what may be translated as 'the great perfect Mirror of Wisdom.'" There are many stages of kensho. See also Satori.

MUSHIN — Literally, this means "no mind" (*mu*, no; *shin*, mind), which means "no ego." It means the mind is in a state of equilibrium.

POSITIVE SAMADHI — Remaining in samadhi while interacting with the world.

PURE EXISTENCE — The state we realize in samadhi, which Katsuki Sekida calls "the zero level of consciousness." As he writes in *Zen Training*, "Although no thought occurs, a bright illumination seemingly lights up the mind. Or rather, the mind itself emits the illumination.... It is not that a light is illuminating the mind but that the mind is illuminating itself. There is nothing to be found: no world, no others, no self, no time. There is only a subtle existence, of which there can be no description." And in the beginning of the chapter titled "Pure Existence" he writes, "The activity of consciousness ... conceals the real nature of existence.... First you have to go through absolute samadhi, where the activity of consciousness is reduced to zero level, and where you can vividly see existence in its nakedness."

PURE SENSATION — When the process of thinking is inhibited, pure sensation results. "Sensations are the first things in the way of consciousness" (William James, *Textbook of Psychology*).

SAMADHI — The state in which the activity of consciousness — including all thought — ceases and an absolute silence and stillness reigns, bathed in a pure, serene light. Usually, when we use the term samadhi, we are referring to absolute samadhi instead of positive samadhi. Katsuki Sekida writes in *Zen Training* (p. 238), "In absolute samadhi the veil is cleared away and the perfect mirror is allowed to appear.... The great Mirror of Wisdom becomes brilliantly lit."

SATORI — The realization of our True Nature sometimes experienced when emerging from absolute samadhi. "Sakyamuni Buddha's satori was a matter of creating a new world.... The unprecedented experience came to him suddenly, striking him like a thunderbolt, and his every problem was solved in an instant" (from *Zen Training*). See also Kensho.

TANDEN — The lower part of the abdomen. Traditionally regarded in the East as the seat of human spiritual power.

ZAZEN — Sitting meditation.

ZEN — Meditation that leads to absolute samadhi while sitting and positive samadhi while interacting with the world.

1. William James, *Textbook of Psychology* (London: Macmillan, 1892), pp. 12–13.

2. Katsuki Sekida, in *Zen Training* (New York and Tokyo: Weatherhill, Inc., 1975), pp. 47–52, goes into this phenomenon of the tension in the tanden stimulating the cortex in great detail; in doing so,

Sekida also draws from Arthur C. Guyton, *Function of the Human Body* (Philadelphia and London: Saunders, 1959), pp. 370–72.

3. This figure and the account of normal respiration are adapted, with modifications, from Arthur C. Guyton, *Function of the Human Body*, pp. 220–21.

4. In the original work, the author goes into fascinating detail: "The *kanna* Zen (working on koans) of the Rinzai sect involves a large element of positive samadhi (although training in absolute samadhi is also found in this school), while in the practice of *shikantaza* of the Soto school, absolute samadhi is more important (though of course here, too, positive samadhi is developed as well)." *Zen Training*, p. 62.

And later he adds, "It seems likely that the two types of samadhi are correlated with distinctly different patterns of electrical activity in the brain," and refers to various studies in India and Japan. *Zen Training*, p. 63.

5. See the Glossary for a more complete definition of kensho. For much greater depth, see Katsuki Sekida's *Zen Training*. There is an entire chapter called "Kensho Experiences."

6. This poem is from Case 5 of the *Hekigan Roku*. The entire book of koans has been brilliantly translated with commentaries by Katsuki Sekida in his great work *Two Zen Classics*.

7. In *Zen Training* (p. 163), Katsuki Sekida comments: "'Thrownness' is a term that appears in Heidegger's *Being and Time*. No one seems to take it as a disease and an object of possible remedy." One time in conversation, Sekida said (this is paraphrased — probably inaccurately — from memory), "Western philosophers, especially the Existentialists, have discovered Buddha's First Great Truth: life is suffering, life is basically unsatisfactory, filled with anxiety. But they haven't gone beyond that, to see there is a state beyond suffering." In other words, they haven't discovered the other three Great Truths of the Buddha. In Zen, we study all four of Buddha's greatest insights: the truth of suffering, its causes, its cessation, and the path to its cessation. In doing so, we go beyond "thrownness."

8. *Hekigan Roku*, Case 94. Quoted from *Two Zen Classics*, translated and with commentaries by Katsuki Sekida.

9. Katsuki Sekida writes in *Zen Training* (p. 174): "Jo Hoshi (A.D. 382–414) was a genius as a Buddhist

scholar. He is said to have met an untimely death by execution when, for religious reasons, he refused to obey an order of the ruler of the state. According to legend, his farewell poem was as follows:

> The four elements have originally no master;
> The five aggregates are essentially empty.
> Now my head meets the sword;
> Let's do it like hewing the spring breeze.

Sekida adds: "On another occasion, Jo wrote, 'The person who has exhausted truth is vast and void, and leaves no trace. All things are one's own making. Those who realize all things as themselves are none other than sages.'"

10. This description includes words from one of the kensho experiences Katsuki Sekida writes about in *Zen Training* (pp. 158–59). He has obviously written from direct experience. Earlier in the book, Sekida wrote that perhaps someday a genius of Zen would appear to be able to describe the Zen experience in writing. I believe he was being modest; this passage as well as many others in his work is in my opinion the work of genius.

"last night, two clay bulls....," 93; "way of Nansen" and, 69–73

Zen Mind, Beginner's Mind (Suzuki Roshi), viii

Zen training (in search of the missing ox): 1. starting the search for the ox, 84–85, *84*, 97–98; 2. finding the footprints, 86, *86*, 98; 3. catching a glimpse of the ox, 87–89, *87*, 95; 4. catching the ox, 89–90, 99–101; 5. taming the ox, 90–91, *90*, 101–2; 6. riding the ox home, 91, *91*, 102–3; 7. ox lost, you remain, 92, *92*, 103–4; 8. no ox, no you, 93–94, *93*, 95, 104–5; 9. returning to the source, 94–96, *94*, 105–6; 10. in town with helping hands, 96, *96*, 106

Zen Training (Sekida), viii, ix–x, 112, 113, 114, 115, 115n. 2, 116n. 4, 116n. 5, 117n. 7

ABOUT THE AUTHOR

KATSUKI SEKIDA (1903–1987) began his Zen practice in 1915 and trained at the Empuku-ji Monastery in Kyoto and the Ryutaku-ji Monastery in Mishima, Japan, where he had deep experience of samadhi early in life. He became a high school teacher of

English until his retirement in 1945, then he returned to full-time study of Zen.

He taught at the Honolulu Zendo and Maui Zendo from 1963 to 1970 and at the London Zen Society from 1970 to 1972. Then he produced his two great works, both published in America and Japan by Weatherhill, Inc.: *Zen Training* in 1975 and *Two Zen Classics* in 1977.